When spring arrives,
The grass awakens,
Flowers bloom,
And swallows fly back home.

When summer comes,
The lotus blooms,
And dragonflies soar.

When autumn arrives,
Chrysanthemums bloom,
Fruits ripen,
And a bountiful harvest brings joy to all.

When winter comes,
The north wind blows,
Snowflakes fall,
And a snowy winter promises a good year ahead.

Sometimes it snows. When it snows, we can build snowmen, roll snowballs, and have snowball fights.

Sometimes the wind blows hard. When it does, the small trees bend in the wind.

On cloudy days, when the sky is full of dark clouds, it rains. When it rains, we wear rain boots and carry umbrellas.

On sunny days, the sun shines, and the warm sunlight feels cozy on our skin.